It's A Fair Swap!

by Mary Miller

Editorial Offices: Glenview, Illinois • Parsippany, New Jersey • New York, New York
Sales Offices: Needham, Massachusetts • Duluth, Georgia • Glenview, Illinois
Coppell, Texas • Ontario, California • Mesa, Arizona

Have you ever traded magazines with a classmate? Have you ever swapped toys? Then you have bartered. Bartering is trading for things we need or want instead of paying for them with money.

A long time ago, people did not use money. They traded for what they wanted or needed. A farmer could trade a bag of grain for some fish. Both traders had to agree that their goods had equal value. If they could not agree, then the trade, or barter, would not happen.

When colonists headed for America, people in Europe were using coin and paper money. But there were no stores in America. The colonists couldn't use their money. They had to gather their own food. They had to make their own clothes.

Bartering is an exchange of items that are equal in value.

The Native Americans used a form of money based on seashells. They also bartered for what they needed. The Native Americans were expert hunters and trappers. They had plenty of animal skins to trade with the colonists.

Some colonists traded with the Native Americans.

Many Europeans wanted the furs that the Native Americans had. At trading posts, the colonists traded goods for animal furs. The Native Americans got things they could not make with their tools such as mirrors, beads, and shirts.

Early colonists also traded with each other. A blacksmith might trade his horseshoeing service with someone who could sew a shirt.

Over time, towns formed. Each town had a general store.

These stores had everything from sewing thread to live chickens.

Farmers traveled from their farms to towns to get supplies. Often they grew extra crops to trade for things they couldn't make or grow.

As the country grew, people began to use money to buy goods. They found money easier to carry to the marketplace than crops or livestock. In payment for a new rug, a carpetmaker preferred a handful of coins to a herd of straying goats!

Later, shopping malls replaced the stores owned by local merchants. By that time, people did little bartering.

Today, goods and services are traded on the Internet. An electrician might trade his knowledge of wires with a carpenter who can fix his roof.

These days money is used more than bartering. Still, bartering is a good way to learn how to trade fairly. Gardening is a service you might trade for a new kite. What services and items could you barter with your friends?